Weekly Reader Children's Book Club presents

# YOU'VE COME A LONG WAY, CHARLIE BROWN

# YOU'VE COME A LONG WAY, CHARLIE BROWN

## A NEW PEANUTS BOOK

### by Charles M. Schulz

**HOLT, RINEHART AND WINSTON**
New York • Chicago • San Francisco

Published simultaneously in Canada by Holt, Rinehart
and Winston of Canada, Limited.

First published in book form in 1971.

Library of Congress Catalog Number: 77-161207

First Edition

ISBN: 0-03-086713-4

Printed in the United States of America

This book is a presentation of
**The Popcorn Bag**
**Weekly Reader Book Club Senior Division**

Weekly Reader Book Division offers book clubs for
children from preschool to young adulthood. All
quality hardcover books are selected by a distinguished
Weekly Reader Selection Board.

For further information write to:
**Weekly Reader Book Division**
1250 Fairwood Avenue
Columbus, Ohio 43216

Weekly Reader Children's Book Club Edition

Publisher's edition: $2.95

THERE'S OUR MAILBOX... WOULDN'T IT BE GREAT IF THERE WAS A VALENTINE IN THERE FOR ME FROM THAT LITTLE RED-HAIRED GIRL?

WOULDN'T IT BE GREAT IF IT WAS A REAL FANCY ONE WITH ALL SORTS OF HEARTS ALL OVER IT AND LACE AND EVERYTHING?

MAYBE IT WILL EVEN BE A SCENTED VALENTINE..IT WILL SMELL SORT OF LIKE VIOLETS OR A RARE PERFUME...

THIS IS SUNDAY, CHARLIE BROWN... THERE'S NO MAIL DELIVERY ON SUNDAY...

*SIGH*

I GOT A VALENTINE FROM JOYCE!

AND I GOT ONE FROM SHIRLEY, AND FROM BARBARA, AND FROM SUE, AND FROM VIRGINIA, AND FROM PAT, AND FROM KAY, AND...

I HATE SOMEONE WHO GLOATS OVER ALL HIS VALENTINES!

THE FIFTEENTH OF FEBRUARY IS ALWAYS "GLOAT DAY"!

---

A Report on George Washington

George Washington was a great man.

He probably had some faults, but if he did, I don't know what they were.

Which is just as well.

MY REPORT IS ON POPULATION CONTROL...

PEOPLE ARE EVERYWHERE.. SOME PEOPLE SAY THERE ARE TOO MANY OF US, BUT NO ONE WANTS TO LEAVE..

WHAT'S SO FUNNY ?!

BY GOLLY, THIS IS A SERIOUS REPORT! YOU'D BETTER STOP LAUGHING!

I DON'T HAVE TO STAND FOR THIS!

I CAN WALK OUT OF THIS SCHOOL, YOU KNOW! I CAN GO TO MY LOCKER AND GET MY COAT AND MY BOOKS AND LEAVE !!

AND THAT'S JUST WHAT I'M GONNA DO! GOOD-BY !!

YES, MA'AM ?

I FORGOT MY LOCKER COMBINATION..

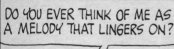

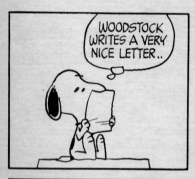

GOOD MORNING, FRED..

HERE'S THE WORLD-FAMOUS GROCERY CLERK TYING HIS APRON AND GETTING READY TO WORK BEHIND THE CHECK-OUT COUNTER..

GOOD MORNING, MRS. BARTLEY... HOW'S YOUR BRIDGE GAME? DID YOU HAVE A NICE WEEKEND?

BREAD.. THIRTY-NINE TWICE... JELLY.. FORTY-NINE... SALAD DRESSING..SIXTY-SEVEN.. THAT IT, SWEETIE?

CARRY OUT

OH, I'M SORRY, MRS. BARTLEY..I DIDN'T MEAN TO STARTLE YOU..

GOOD MORNING MRS. LOCKHART.. HOW ARE YOU TODAY? HOW'S ALL THE FAMILY?

PICKLES.. SIXTY.. BREAD.. THIRTY-NINE THRICE.. EGGS.. FIFTY-NINE TWICE ..CARROTS..

HEY, FRED, HOW MUCH ON THE CARROTS?
DID YOU HAVE ANY BOTTLES, MRS. LOCKHART? THANK YOU

GOOD MORNING, MRS. MENDELSON.. HAS YOUR HUSBAND FOUND A JOB YET? HOW WAS YOUR TRIP TO HAWAII?

BREAD.. THIRTY-NINE EIGHT TIMES.. SOUP.. TWO FOR TWENTY-NINE ...TEN CANS... COFFEE.. A DOLLAR SEVENTY-EIGHT... TUNA ..THIRTY-NINE TWICE..

⁂ SIGH ⁂ SEVEN HOURS AND FORTY MINUTES TO GO... GOOD MORNING, MRS. ALBO..HOW ARE YOU TODAY..SWEETIE?

HERE, CHARLIE BROWN... SIGN THIS PETITION!

WHAT'S IT FOR?

DON'T BE SO WISHY-WASHY.. JUST SIGN IT!

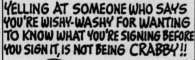

WANTING TO KNOW WHAT YOU'RE SIGNING IS NOT BEING WISHY-WASHY!

WHY ARE YOU SO CRABBY?

YELLING AT SOMEONE WHO SAYS YOU'RE WISHY-WASHY FOR WANTING TO KNOW WHAT YOU'RE SIGNING BEFORE YOU SIGN IT, IS NOT BEING CRABBY!!

ALL RIGHT, IF I LET YOU READ IT, WILL YOU SIGN IT?

"WE, THE UNDERSIGNED, THINK OUR MANAGER IS TOO WISHY-WASHY AND TOO CRABBY"

YOU PROMISED TO SIGN IT..

I'M THE ONLY PERSON I KNOW WHO'S EVER SIGNED A PETITION AGAINST HIMSELF

RATS!

ALL WEEK LONG I'VE LOOKED FORWARD TO THIS GAME, AND NOW IT'S STARTING TO RAIN!

ACTUALLY, THIS RAIN IS GOOD FOR THE CARROTS, CHARLIE BROWN, AND IT'S GOOD FOR THE BEANS AND BARLEY, AND THE OATS AND THE ALFALFA...

OR IS IT BAD FOR THE ALFALFA? I THINK IT'S GOOD FOR THE SPINACH AND BAD FOR THE APPLES..IT'S GOOD FOR THE BEETS AND THE ORANGES...

IT'S BAD FOR THE GRAPES, BUT GOOD FOR THE BARBERS, BUT BAD FOR THE CARPENTERS, BUT GOOD FOR THE COUNTY OFFICIALS, BUT BAD FOR THE CAR DEALERS, BUT...

*SIGH*

RATS! I CAN'T STAND LOSING ALL THE TIME!

THERE MUST BE SOMETHING WRONG WITH ME...

I USED TO COME HOME AND HURL MY GLOVE INTO THE CLOSET..

NOW, I CAN'T EVEN HIT THE CLOSET!

I CAN'T BELIEVE IT! HE THINKS THAT I THINK I'M BETTER THAN HE IS!

THAT'S THE BEST THING ANYONE HAS EVER SAID TO ME! KEEP THE GLOVE, THIBAULT! YOU'VE DONE ME A GREAT FAVOR!

I DON'T UNDERSTAND YOU, CHUCK!

YOU SURE KNOW SOME WEIRD PEOPLE..

YOU THINK HE'S WEIRD? YOU SHOULD SEE HIS FUNNY-LOOKING FRIEND WITH THE BIG NOSE!

SO I JUST LET HIM KEEP THE GLOVE..

MAYBE I WAS AFRAID TO FIGHT HIM... I DON'T KNOW... I DON'T EVEN REALLY CARE.. THE MAIN THING IS, I FELT BETTER...

I'M PROUD OF YOU, CHARLIE BROWN.. NOW, MAYBE YOU'LL BE ABLE TO START FACING SOME OF LIFE'S PROBLEMS ON THE "GUT LEVEL"..

THAT'S A MEDICAL TERM

IT WOULD SOUND MORE CONVINCING IF YOU WEREN'T HOLDING THAT BLANKET!

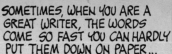

SOMETIMES, WHEN YOU ARE A GREAT WRITER, THE WORDS COME SO FAST YOU CAN HARDLY PUT THEM DOWN ON PAPER...

SOMETIMES

I HAVE A SUGGESTION FOR YOU..

IF YOU CAN'T SELL YOUR NOVEL, WHY NOT TRY A BIOGRAPHY? PICK OUT SOME PERSON YOU LIKE AND WRITE HIS LIFE STORY...

THAT MIGHT BE KIND OF HARD

WE DOGS DON'T LIKE ANYONE!

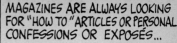

SOMETIMES, WHEN I'M OUT HERE ON THE MOUND PITCHING, A VERY PECULIAR THING HAPPENS..

SOMETIMES I START THINKING ABOUT THAT LITTLE RED-HAIRED GIRL..

HERE I AM, SURROUNDED BY KIDS PLAYING BASEBALL..EVERYONE IS YELLING AND SCREAMING AND RUNNING AROUND, AND WHAT AM I DOING? I'M PITCHING, BUT I'M THINKING ABOUT HER

I'M THINKING ABOUT HOW I'LL PROBABLY NEVER SEE HER AGAIN, AND ABOUT HOW UNFAIR IT IS, AND I FEEL LIKE SITTING DOWN AND CRYING...

I STAND OUT HERE, AND I THROW THE BALL, AND I THINK ABOUT HOW HAPPY I COULD BE IF I WERE HER FRIEND, AND IF I COULD BE WITH HER, AND SHE LIKED ME..AND...

SOMETIMES I ALMOST FORGET WHERE I AM...

GET THE BALL OVER THE PLATE, YOU BLOCKHEAD!

ALMOST

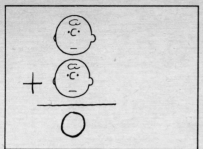

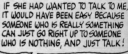

THAT'S LIFE... YOU SET YOUR ALARM FOR SIX O'CLOCK, AND THE WORM SETS HIS FOR FIVE-THIRTY

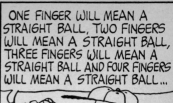

ONE FINGER WILL MEAN A STRAIGHT BALL, TWO FINGERS WILL MEAN A STRAIGHT BALL, THREE FINGERS WILL MEAN A STRAIGHT BALL AND FOUR FINGERS WILL MEAN A STRAIGHT BALL...

I HAVE A VERY SARCASTIC CATCHER

CAN THINKING BAD THOUGHTS CAUSE IT TO RAIN?

LINUS TOOK THE LAST DOUGHNUT THIS MORNING, AND I YELLED AT HIM, AND NOW IT'S CLOUDING UP, SO I WAS JUST WONDERING...

IF BAD THOUGHTS CAUSED RAIN, WE'D NEVER SEE THE SUN SHINE

PLAY BALL!

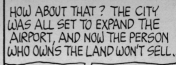

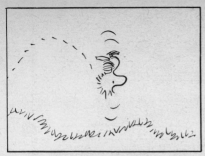

AS LONG AS THIS IS GOING TO BE A FOURTH OF JULY SPEECH, I THINK I SHOULD SLIP IN A FEW DIGS ABOUT DOGS NOT BEING ALLOWED TO VOTE..WE CAN BE DRAFTED INTO THE ARMY, BUT WE CAN'T VOTE...

HMM

THEN I'LL TELL MY LATEST ANTI-CAT JOKE..THE DOG AUDIENCE WILL LOVE THIS ONE...HEE HEE HEE HEE HEE!

I HAVE THE WORLD'S LARGEST COLLECTION OF ANTI-CAT JOKES!

THERE HE GOES... OFF TO GIVE HIS FOURTH OF JULY SPEECH TO THE DOGS AT THE DAISY HILL PUPPY FARM..

HAS HE BEEN REHEARSING WHAT HE'S GOING TO SAY?

OH, YES...THAT'S ALL HE'S BEEN THINKING ABOUT LATELY..

"AS WE ARE GATHERED HERE TODAY ON THIS SOLEMN OCCASION, I AM REMINDED OF A RATHER AMUSING STORY..."

The

It

OKAY, WHAT SHALL WE READ TONIGHT ..."TREASURE ISLAND"? "HANS BRINKER"?

"THE SIX BUNNY-WUNNIES AND THEIR PONY CART".... AGAIN ?!?

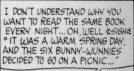

I DON'T UNDERSTAND WHY YOU WANT TO READ THE SAME BOOK EVERY NIGHT... OH, WELL ≠SIGH≠ "IT WAS A WARM SPRING DAY, AND THE SIX BUNNY-WUNNIES DECIDED TO GO ON A PICNIC..."

"'I'LL FIX THE LUNCH', SAID PAM BUNNY-WUNNIE..'I'LL HITCH UP OUR PONY,' SAID PETER BUNNY-WUN...':

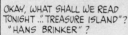

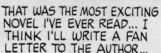

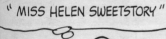

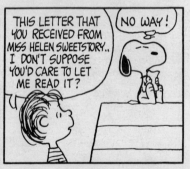

GUESS WHAT I FOUND...

IT'S A MAGAZINE PHOTO-STORY ABOUT YOUR FAVORITE AUTHOR... NOW, YOU'LL GET THE CHANCE TO SEE WHAT SHE LOOKS LIKE :.

"MISS HELEN SWEETSTORY, AUTHOR OF THE BUNNY-WUNNIE SERIES, RELAXES HERE IN A PORCH SWING SURROUNDED BY HER TWENTY-FOUR PET..............

....CATS "!

THANKS AGAIN FOR THE BOOKS

YOU'RE WELCOME.. FORGET IT... GOOD RIDDANCE..

SNOOPY GAVE ME ALL HIS "BUNNY-WUNNIE" BOOKS

WHEN HE FOUND OUT THAT HELEN SWEETSTORY OWNS TWENTY-FOUR CATS, HE STOPPED READING HER BOOKS

BACK TO HERMANN HESSE

QUESTION NUMBER ONE...
WHAT IS THE CAPITAL OF
CAMEROUN?

*Answer: When I grow up, I am going to be a hair dresser, and hair dressers obviously don't have to know such things.*

QUESTION NUMBER TWO...
WHAT IS THE LENGTH OF
THE RIO GRANDE RIVER?

*Answer: When I grow up, I will also probably be a housewife, and could not care less about the length of the Rio Grande river.*

QUESTION NUMBER THREE... WHAT IS THE
NAME OF THE LARGEST PYRAMID?

*Answer: When I grow up, I will undoubtedly be a member of the smart set.*

*We members of the smart set rarely discuss such things as pyramids.*

THIS IS AN
EASY TEST..

Theme: On Returning to School After Summer Vacation.

No one can deny the joys of a summer vacation with its days of warmth and freedom!

It must be admitted, however, that the true joy lies in returning to our halls of learning.

Is not life itself a learning process? Do we not mature according to our learning? Do not each of us desire that he

YES, MA'AM? OH... WHY, THANK YOU.. I'M GLAD YOU LIKED IT..

AS THE YEARS GO BY, YOU LEARN WHAT SELLS!

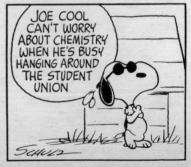

ONE, PLEASE..

YOU KNOW WHAT I'M DOING, LINUS? I'M PRETENDING THAT YOU'RE TAKING ME TO THE MOVIES..

WELL, I'M **NOT**! WE JUST HAPPEN TO BE STANDING IN THE SAME LINE!

I'M PRETENDING THAT YOU CALLED ME UP AND SAID, "HOW WOULD YOU LIKE TO GO TO THE MOVIES?" AND I SAID, "OH, THAT WOULD BE NICE..THANK YOU VERY MUCH FOR ASKING ME!"

AND THEN I'M PRETENDING THAT YOU CAME BY TO PICK ME UP, AND WE WALKED DOWN HERE TOGETHER...

WELL, YOU CAN STOP PRETENDING BECAUSE IT'S NEVER GOING TO HAPPEN ...ONE, PLEASE!

ALL RIGHT, JUST FOR THAT, I'M GOING TO TAKE WHOEVER IS STANDING BEHIND ME IN LINE!!

GO RIGHT AHEAD

ONE, PLEASE!

✳SIGH✳

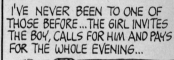

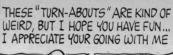

Columbus Day
by Sally Brown

THIS IS A REPORT FOR SCHOOL

I SEE

Columbus Day was a very brave man. He wanted to sail around the world.

"I can give you three ships, Mr. Day," said the Queen.

GOOD LUCK

THANK YOU

SCHULZ

I LIKE A WALK ON A BRISK FALL DAY..

AFTERWARD, IT'S FUN TO COME HOME AND HAVE A CUP OF HOT CHOCOLATE..

AND SIT IN FRONT OF A WARM TV

SCHULZ

HALLOWEEN IS OVER..

HAVE YOU BEEN SITTING OUT IN THAT PUMPKIN PATCH ALL NIGHT AGAIN?

I WAS WAITING FOR THE GREAT PUMPKIN...HE DIDN'T COME..

WHY DON'T YOU JUST CURSE THE GREAT PUMPKIN, AND FORGET THE WHOLE THING?

YOU SOUND LIKE JOB'S WIFE

SHAKE YOUR FIST IN THE AIR, AND SAY, "CURSE YOU, GREAT PUMPKIN! I KNOW YOU DON'T EXIST!"

THEN YOU'D BE **FREE**! YOU CAN DO IT!!

JUST SAY, "CURSE YOU, GREAT PUMPKIN! I KNOW YOU DON'T EXIST! I DON'T NEED YOU! I'M FREE! I'M FREE!"

COME ON, YOU CAN DO IT! JUST SAY IT!

COME ON! SAY IT!

JUST WAIT 'TIL NEXT YEAR!!

OH, GOOD GRIEF!

The Ocean - A report.

The ocean is full of water. "Ha!" You may say. "What else?" That's a good question.

SOMETIMES IT'S EASY TO GET BOGGED DOWN ON THESE REPORTS

THIS IS MY REPORT ON THE OCEANS OF THE WORLD

" THERE ARE NO OCEANS IN KANSAS.. THERE ARE NO OCEANS IN NEBRASKA.. THERE ARE NO OCEANS IN NEVADA.. THERE ARE NO OCEANS IN MINNESOTA.. "

" THERE ARE NO OCEANS IN IOWA.. THERE ARE.. "

I THOUGHT YOU WANTED US TO GO IN TO DETAIL ...

Book report: Ethan Frome

Not being a married person, I think it is impossible for me to understand the emotions involved in this novel.

THAT'S YOUR BOOK REPORT?

SURE

YES, MA'AM? WHY, THANK YOU... I'M GLAD WE AGREE..

YOU HAVE TO LEARN TO TELL IT LIKE IT IS, CHARLIE BROWN..

SCHULZ

"The Cabin"

Chapter One

When he got up that morning, the sky was clear.

By now, however, it had turned gray. He shivered slightly.

Soon it began to snow.

At first, only a few feathers swirling in the wind.

Then heavy, wet flakes which quickly covered everything.

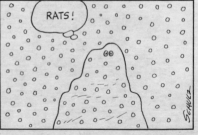

RATS!

COOL AND CALM..

HERE'S THE WORLD FAMOUS HOCKEY PLAYER SKATING OUT FOR THE FACE-OFF...

GET THE PUCK!

PASS! SHOOT! CHECK 'IM!

KNOCK HIM DOWN! SHOOT! CLEAR IT! MOVE! SKATE WITH IT!

HIT HIM! SHOOT!!

SKATE! SKATE! ALLONS! ALLONS!

A WHISTLE!

WHO, ME??!

TWO MINUTES FOR TRIPPING, TWO MINUTES FOR ELBOWING, TWO MINUTES FOR SLASHING, TWO MINUTES FOR HIGH-STICKING, TWO MINUTES FOR CHARGING, TWO MINUTES FOR HOLDING, TWO MINUTES FOR CROSS CHECKING, FIVE MINUTES FOR BOARD CHECKING AND A TEN-MINUTE MISCONDUCT...

BUT I'M SUCH A NICE GUY...

SCHULZ

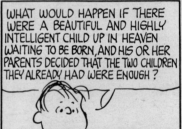

BEETHOVEN WAS BORN ON DEC. 16, 1770

THAT WAS A GOOD YEAR..THAT WAS THE SAME YEAR THAT GAINSBOROUGH PAINTED "THE BLUE BOY"

MAYBE WE'LL HAVE ANOTHER YEAR LIKE THAT PRETTY SOON

I HOPE SO...WE'RE OVERDUE

"AS A YOUNG BOY, BEETHOVEN WAS POWERFULLY BUILT"

"HE WAS SHORT OF STATURE, HAD BROAD SHOULDERS, A SHORT NECK, A LARGE HEAD AND A ROUND NOSE"

HE SOUNDS KIND OF CUTE

BEETHOVEN WAS NOT CUTE !!

---

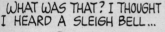

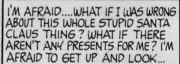

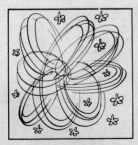

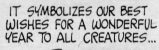

YOU'RE GOING TO BE PROUD OF ME, LUCY... I'VE DECIDED THAT THIS NEXT YEAR IS GOING TO BE MY YEAR OF DECISION!

THIS IS A LIST OF THINGS IN MY LIFE THAT I'M GOING TO CORRECT.. I'M GOING TO BE A BETTER PERSON!

NOT ME... I'M GOING TO SPEND THIS WHOLE YEAR REGRETTING THE PAST..IT'S THE ONLY WAY, CHARLIE BROWN..

I'M GOING TO CRY OVER SPILT MILK, AND SIGH OVER LOST LOVES...

IT'S A LOT EASIER..IT'S TOO HARD TO IMPROVE.. I TRIED IT ONCE... IT DROVE ME CRAZY..

"FORGET THE FUTURE" IS MY MOTTO.. REGRET THE PAST! OH, HOW I REGRET THE PAST!

WHY DID I DO THIS? WHY DID I DO THAT? WHY? I REGRET IT ALL!

OH, WHAT REGRETS! WHAT REMORSE! WHAT ANGUISH! WHAT...

* SIGH *